FRONT RANGE SINGLE TRACKS 2

THE BEST SINGLE-TRACK TRAILS NEAR DENVER AND BOULDER

by Tom Barnhart

ISBN-10: 0-9638419-0-4
ISBN-13: 978-0-9638419-0-2

Printed in the United States of America

MOUNTAIN BIKING IS A CHALLENGING SPORT. IT IS THE INDIVIDUAL RIDER'S RESPONSIBILITY TO TRAVEL AT A SAFE SPEED WITHIN ONE'S ABILITIES AND WITHIN THE GIVEN TRAIL CONDITIONS. THE AUTHOR IS NOT ENCOURAGING OR RECOMMENDING RIDING A SPECIFIC RIDE LISTED IN THIS BOOK. DUE TO CHANGING TRAIL CONDITIONS IT IS HIGHLY RECOMMENDED THAT ONE CONSULT THE U.S. FOREST SERVICE OR LOCAL BIKE SHOPS PRIOR TO ATTEMPTING A RIDE. THE AUTHOR OF THIS GUIDE CANNOT BE HELD RESPONSIBLE FOR ACCIDENT OR INJURY ARISING FROM THESE RIDES OR THE SPORT OF MOUNTAIN BIKING.

4th Printing

Fat Tire Press
P.O. Box 620283
Littleton, Colorado 80162

barno@excite.com

CONTENTS

Goofing Around in Buffalo Creek

ACKNOWLEDGMENTS

During the writing of this book, I was assisted and supported by a great number of individuals and organizations who gave their advice, suggestions and time for this endeavor. Without them this book could not have been produced.

Special thanks to Scott Laudenslager of KIMCO for the printing; Jefferson County Open Space staff for their maps; Rick Garnder of Golden Gate Canyon State Park for use of the park map and his valuable thoughts; Scott Dollus of the Pike National Forest for his comments and ride suggestions; Bill and Mary Kay Stoehr of Trails Illustrated Inc. for use of their maps; Trail TopoGraphics for GPS data, Photosynthesis Studio for photo on page 8, Boulder County Parks and Open Space, City of Boulder Open Space Department; US Geological Service; Jason Lampitt, Patty Lee, Steve Levin, Tim Nichols for contributing their valuable comments; Rich Marchbanks for the photos of me; Photosynthesis Studio and NZ Graphics for the cover design; Seven Cycles; riding wizards Randy McLean, Chuck Dufield, Bruce Scott and Russ Crystal; the members of the various mountain biking clubs who keep the trails maintained.

Also, Pikabike, Stever, Ichabod, Godzilla, Lidarman, bobcat and other MTBR Passionites

Entering The Buffalo Creek Burn Area

INTRODUCTION

This guide book introduces the mountain biking community to more rides along the Front Range of Colorado. The Front Range is well suited for fat tire fans because of the wealth of trails, wide varieties of trail terrain, the not overly steep mountains and foothills, and short drive distances from population centers. We along the Front Range are spoiled with the many riding opportunities available to us. Hopefully, the guide book will help you choose the right trail to make for a wonderful day of riding.

Single track rides for all abilities are listed in this book. Every ride contains some single-track trail. The single-track experience is the pinnacle of mountain biking. Every mountain biker should experience the thrill of tightly spaced trees hugging the trail's edge.

This guidebook takes off where my first guide, Front Range Single Tracks, leaves off and adds more of the best single track trails. However many trails are yet to be found and explored. Do not be afraid to break ground and find new rides. Rides can come and go, or change, due to changing land ownership, Mother Nature's wrath or a host of other reasons. Please let me know what is happening to existing rides and potential new rides, so future updates to this book can contain the best possible information. Email me at barno@excite.com.

RIDE PREPARATION

I cannot stress the importance of being prepared for the day's ride. Any trip can be a potential disaster, if you are not prepared to deal with emergencies. How you deal with the problems encountered on the ride will determine whether the ride will turn out all right or not.

MENTAL PREPARATION: Preparation is not just making sure your equipment is in shape, but also whether you are physically and mentally prepared for riding. If you are physically drained or hurt, select an easier ride or sit out the day. Rest and recovery are just as important as riding itself. If you are not mentally into a ride, do something else that day. Remember, we mountain bike to have fun.

BIKE PREPARATION: The old saying of "an ounce of prevention is worth a pound of cure" applies to mountain biking. Before each ride, spin the wheels making sure the brake pads do not rub the rims. Make sure the seat height is properly adjusted and the gears shift smoothly. Check that the tires are properly inflated and remember to carry your pump and water bottles. Cleaning the bike and lubricating the chain after several rides will prolong the life of the bike. An annual tune-up by a qualified bike repair professional is a wise investment and will save money later.

SEAT PACK ESSENTIALS: Carrying the right necessities under your seat

and knowing how to use them can save many a day. At a minimum, carry the following:
1. patch kit, spare tube and tire levers
2. 6" crescent wrench, needle nose pliers
3. small phillips-head and flathead screwdrivers
4. chain tool and several spare links
5. complete set of allen wrenches
6. small amount of duct tape wrapped around a pencil
7. waterproof matches
8. pocket knife
9. quarters for a pay phone
10. spoke wrench
11. small bottle of insect repellent

This may sound like a lot of junk rattling around under your seat, and it is, but I would rather ride with tools than walk without them. The two most used items have been the insect repellent and surprisingly, the chain tool. If you do not own or know how to use the tools listed above, ride with someone who does. It does not do much good to have the tools and have no idea how to use them. Therefore, I recommend taking a repair/maintenance class to learn how to field fix your bike.

CLOTHING: Weather can change rapidly in the high country, so be prepared. Take a rain jacket or wind breaker and dress in layers. A small fanny or hip pack is ideal to carry not only extra clothing, but also a place to hold your lunch and extra water. A pair of cycling gloves protects against abrasions during falls and helps to avoid blisters. Lycra padded bike shorts reduce seat chaffing and make for a more comfortable ride. Don't forget the sunglasses, preferably with 100% UV protection, lip balm and the sunscreen. ALWAYS WEAR YOUR HELMET!

TRAIL CONDITIONS: The final ride preparation item is to check out the trail conditions before you depart. Inquire with the friendly Forest Service personnel, Open Space staff or a bike shop about current trail conditions and possible trail closures.

RIDE ETHICS

If mountain bikers do not adhere to ethical riding behavior, we risk losing access to existing and future trails. With the ever-expanding number of users visiting the national forests, state parks and open space, we must learn how to share the trail with other users and prevent conflicts. Here are a few common rules you should adhere to:
1. Ride in control. Save the speed for the professional race courses.
2. Wilderness areas prohibit mountain bikes. It is tempting, but don't!
3. Avoid spooking livestock and wildlife. Slow to walking speed.
4. Respect private properties and no trespassing signs.
5. Leave gates as you found them.

6. Obey all traffic regulations and use hand signals in traffic.
7. Pack litter out, even someone else's trash.
8. Stay on the trail. Do not shortcut switchbacks.
9. Avoid biking alone. Let someone know where you are going.
10. Avoid riding on muddy trails.
11. Yield to hikers, horses and uphill mountain bikers.
12. Offer help to bikers in need. What goes around comes around.
13. If you are dumb enough to bike through hunting areas during rifle season, at least wear blaze orange.

Finally, give something back to the sport of mountain biking. Volunteer to improve trails and access. Join a local mountain biking club. A list of them can be found on page 57. Get politically active and make sure mountain biker's needs are heard when trail issues come before political bodies.

SOME PARTING POINTS TO PONDER

1. Conditioning and biking experience beat bicycle technology.
2. Sliding is for baseball, not mountain biking.
3. A dirty bike is a sign of a clean mind and a fun day's ride.
4. Expect to go the wrong way at times.
5. Yield to the stupid biker for your own safety.
6. A bike path is inherently more dangerous than single-track trail.
7. If you fail to clean a section, try the section again.
8. Expect to fall off your bike and draw blood.
9. Braking gets you in trouble, momentum less so.
10. If someone says the trail was a "piece of cake", it probably wasn't.
11. Never get separated from your water or your lunch.

Bikes are free!

HOW TO USE THIS GUIDE

For each ride, a standard format is used so you can compare and contrast the different rides and then select the ride that matches your personal abilities and desires for the day. Nothing is worse than struggling along a trail beyond your limits because of a lack of knowledge about the ride. This book will provide sufficient information to help make an informed decision for the day's ride. Each ride contains information on ride distance, technical and physical difficulty, trail surfaces encountered, elevation gain, directions to the trailhead, ride description, optional routes, hill profile, and of course a map of the ride's route. A ride difficulty rating follows this section. No estimated time for completing a trip is given due to the wide range of biking abilities, rest requirements and potential optional mileage. The rides are listed alphabetically. Below is a further explanation of each section meaning.

DISTANCE: Most ride distances are measured as round trip, except where noted. The distance for each ride was determined from a cyclocomputer and/or GPS data rounded to the nearest tenth of a mile. Although the mileage is accurate, some errors may regrettably exist.

Mileage is mentioned in the ride description, at trail splits and landmarks, as a help to stay oriented and to simply to let you know how far you have progressed. Mileage is shown in **bold**. Obviously a cyclocomputer will enhance the use of the guide book, but with the sufficient description of landmarks along the way, a cyclocomputer is not required.

DIFFICULTY RATING: Some ride guides have developed detailed difficulty rating scales based on riding skills, distances, elevation changes and types of terrain. Unfortunately, a large degree of rating subjectivity remains because of the skills and conditioning of the individual riders. Therefore, the difficulty levels indicate only a general idea of what can be expected along the trail and the required level of technical and physical abilities. I decided not to make a science project out of the difficulty rating, but did break it into two components: physical and technical difficulty, with each of the components having three categories: easy, moderate and advanced. The trails are rated against one another not only in this guide, but also my first trail guide to determine the final difficulty. The three categories are shown by one, two or three chain rings. A trail with a difficulty rating between categories is shown with an additional half chain ring. The meaning of each of the difficulty ratings is listed on the next page.

	Physical Difficulty	Technical Difficulty
Easy ✿	• less than 6 miles elevation gain • less than 1,000 feet elevation gain • short gradual climbs	• smooth hardpack with few obstacles • basic handling skills
Moderate ✿✿	• 6-15 miles • elevation gain of 1,000 to 1,500 feet • steep grades, but not extended	• rough trail surface • solid biking skills • some obstacles
Advanced ✿✿✿	• greater than 10 miles • elevation gain over 1,500 feet • very steep	• rocky trail surface • large obstacles to negotiate • expert handling skills required

In some cases a ride may progress from one difficulty category to another and generally will show the more difficult rating. One last item: the difficulty ratings are based only on the described direction of the ride. A ride in the opposite direction may have an entirely different rating.

TERRAIN: This section describes the type of trail surfaces to be encountered.

ELEVATION GAIN: Estimated elevation gained between the start of the ride and the finish of the ride. The gain considers only extended gains and not smaller climbs. Total gain for the trip is likely to be higher when shorter rises are included. The gain was estimated from topographic maps, GPS data and/or from a cyclometer with altimeter function.

HILL PROFILE: The elevation profile shows the distribution of climbing and descending over the trip and is a good indicator of when an elevation gain or loss will likely be encountered along the ride. Elevation calculations were taken every half mile or at points where the trail significantly drops or climbs. Ascents and descents between the half mile points on the profile are not shown, but may be included in the elevation gain total. **Please note that the elevation and distance scales may vary between rides, so be careful comparing rides.**

ACCESS: The access description provides the directions to the start of a ride. Directions generally start from a major thoroughfare in or near a Front Range city. Every ride in the book can be driven to with a normal passenger vehicle. Four wheel drive vehicles are not required to reach any of the trailheads.

DESCRIPTION: The introductory paragraph for each ride gives an overall summary of what can be expected and the type of rider who may like the trail. The second description section contains the detail description from the start of the trailhead through completion of the ride. **Read the entire route description before starting a ride so as to avoid surprises such as a creek fording.** The route description is good only for the direction stated.

Included in the descriptions are mileage estimates (indicated in **bold**) to determine approximately how far one has progressed into the ride. Key landmarks such as gates, creek crossings, signs and natural features are used to help the rider follow a route, as are changes in trail conditions, direction and elevation. Use the map frequently in conjunction with the description to determine your course and the number of miles ridden. Changes to a ride can occur due to Mother Nature, trail maintenance, trail rerouting, new roads, sign vandalism and a host of other reasons. You should be prepared for these changes.

TRAIL OPTIONS: This section provides additional riding options. These generally add further mileage off the main trail route. In some cases, the option can be ridden as a separate ride.

MAP: The map included for each ride is either from a USGS 7.5 minutes quadrangle, Trails Illustrated topographic map, Trails TopoGraphics map, State Park map or Open Space map. Each map has a trailhead symbol noted by an asterisk (*), north arrow, route direction and other relevant comments. The basic route is indicated as a solid line; optional rides are indicated, where appropriate, with a dashed line.

It is highly recommended that you carry a complete map of the area in addition to the ride guide map. Trails Illustrated maps are reasonably priced, the most up to date, waterproof and tearproof, and therefore recommended for the Front Range. Trails Illustrated maps can also be useful to explore new rides not found in this guide. Don't leave home without one!

TRAIL RANKINGS

Trail	Name	Physical Difficulty	Technical Difficulty	Miles	Elevation Gain
11.	Lair O' The Bear	O	O	2.0 miles	160 feet
4.	Dell Gulch	O	O	9.6 miles	1,070 feet
6.	Flying J	O	OC	4.0 miles	360 feet
13.	Maxwell Falls	O	OC	4.3 miles	1,000 feet
9.	Heil Ranch	OC	O	7.6 miles	1,000 feet
20.	South Table Mountain	OC	O	9.7 miles	1,060 feet
21.	South Valley Park	OC	OC	6.9 miles	970 feet
14.	Meyers Ranch	OC	OC	4.7 miles	900 feet
16.	Pence to Lair	OO	OC	10.2 miles	2,250 feet
12.	Lower Gashouse	OO	OC	16.2 miles	1,700 feet
15.	Morrison Creek	OO	OC	17.0 miles	1,690 feet
2.	Blue Dot	OO	OO	10.8 miles	1,890 feet
22.	Stevens Gulch	OOC	OO	10.0 miles	2,000 feet
3.	Colorado Trail - South Platte West	OOC	OO	12.6 miles	2,400 feet
19.	Ringtail Trail	OOC	OO	15.8 miles	3,900 feet
5.	Five Parks	OOC	OO	22.5 miles	3,450 feet
1.	Black Bear Trail	OOC	OOC	9.4 miles	1,900 feet
18.	Rattlesnake Gulch	OOC	OOC	7.6 miles	1,350 feet
8.	Golden Gate West	OOC	OOO	10.5 miles	2,000 feet
17.	Pine Valley Loop	OOO	OO	19.2 miles	2,600 feet
7.	Georgia Pass	OOO	OO	23.0 miles	4,000 feet
10.	Indian Creek Loop	OOO	OOC	14.6 miles	2,500 feet

Heading Home

RIDE 1 BLACK BEAR

DISTANCE: 9.4 miles

PHYSICAL: ◯◯◖

TECHNICAL: ◯◯◖

TERRAIN: Very rocky to smooth single track

GAIN: 1,900 feet

MAP: Jefferson County Open Space - Deer Creek

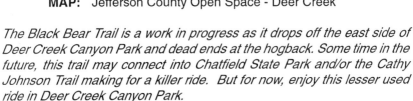

The Black Bear Trail is a work in progress as it drops off the east side of Deer Creek Canyon Park and dead ends at the hogback. Some time in the future, this trail may connect into Chatfield State Park and/or the Cathy Johnson Trail making for a killer ride. But for now, enjoy this lesser used ride in Deer Creek Canyon Park.

ACCESS: From C470, exit at Kipling Street and head south then west following the signs to the Deer Creek Canyon Park entrance.

DESCRIPTION: Begin climbing on the red soiled Plymouth Creek Trail as it rolls for the first few tenths of a mile through the scrub oak. Upon reaching Plymouth Creek **(0.3)**, tackle a tough series of short, rocky climbs before the trail flattens and reaches the Meadowlark Trail **(1.1)**. Here begins the steep "killer" section which when combined with loose surface, makes for a hike-a-bike for most riders. At Plymouth Mountain Trail **(1.6)**, turn left on smoother and narrower trail and head east with some gorgeous views along the way. As you begin dropping, Black Bear Trail will appear on your left **(2.4)**. Take Black Bear Trail and continue the fast drop to the valley floor. After crossing a narrow bridge, find yourself at a paved road **(3.8)**. Turn right and continue east on the paved road towards the hogback for a short distance where the trail resumes and parallels the fenced Lockheed Martin Waterton facility. Upon reaching the hogback, the trail abruptly ends **(4.7)**. Turn around and return via the same route.

TRAIL OPTION: A nice addition to this ride is to climb to the top of Plymouth Mountain. After climbing out of the valley turn left on Plymouth Mtn Trail and continue to crank uphill to Scenic View Trail. Turn right on Scenic View and pedal a short distance to the top of Plymouth Mountain. To return, reverse your course. This will add about 2.6 miles to the overall mileage.

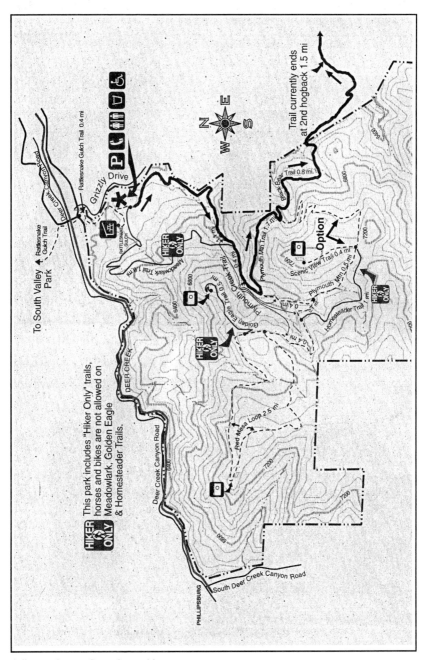

This park includes "Hiker Only" trails, horses and bikes are not allowed on Meadowlark, Golden Eagle & Homesteader Trails.

Jefferson County Open Space Map

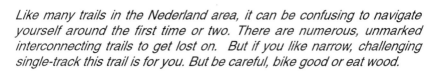

RIDE 2 BLUE DOT

DISTANCE: 10.8 miles

PHYSICAL: ○○

TECHNICAL: ○○

TERRAIN: Paved road; rocky to smooth single and two-track; some difficult technical sections

GAIN: 1,890 feet

MAP: Trails Illustrated Map - Indian Peaks/Gold Hill

Like many trails in the Nederland area, it can be confusing to navigate yourself around the first time or two. There are numerous, unmarked interconnecting trails to get lost on. But if you like narrow, challenging single-track this trail is for you. But be careful, bike good or eat wood.

ACCESS: From Boulder, head west on Canyon (Colorado 119) to Nederland. At the traffic circle, head south (left) on Colorado 119/72 a couple of blocks and look for the old railroad cars and Happy Trails Bicycle shop. The ride begins in this shopping center. Denver riders may want to get to Nederland via Coal Creek Canyon (Colorado 72) to avoid Boulder traffic.

DESCRIPTION: Cut across the parking lot and pickup Big Spring Drive which lies to the south. Climb on Big Spring Drive to where it sharply switchbacks to the right **(1.0)** and find the start of the single track. A short climb brings one to a natural gas pump station **(1.2)** and Magnolia Road. Go left or east and hookup with the narrow Reboot Trail (Do not go into the dump). The narrow Reboot Trail winds its way north and east and spills you out in Reynolds Park **(2.4)**. Turn left downhill and then straight uphill following the power poles. Take the next, more used, right trail spur **(2.6)** and exit from the Reynolds Park with a quick narrow climb to a "T" inter-section. Turn left and then quickly right again at yet another trail intersection. After dropping through some small tight pines you come to another trail intersection **(3.3)**. Turn left and drop into the meadow, now on the Blue Dot trail. From here the trail gets more technical with some hiking likely. Emerge from the forest into a small meadow where the trail divides **(5.2)**. Go right and then quickly right again to a small ridge. Begin drop-ping on some fun double-track to a gate **(6.2)** then via road to the trailhead for Front Range Trails **(6.4)**. Turn right on Magnolia Road and crank gen-erally uphill. Near mile 8.4 spy a gate on the right and Road 606 sign. Now a decision; one has the option of accessing back to the single track system here or to continue on the road. If you continue on the road, crank back to the natural gas pump station **(9.6)**. Turn right and reverse your course back to town.

TRAIL OPTIONS: A. The Dot "System" has many more miles to explore (the trails are shown as dotted lines on the map). Just try them out. **B.** A cute half mile trail connector (Boot Trail) heads west from the natural gas station and connects to the West Magnolia trails. Blue Dot and West Magnolia can be combined for a day of mighty fine riding. **C.** Instead of climbing back on Magnolia Road, you can reverse yourself on the single track for more fun. Like duh.

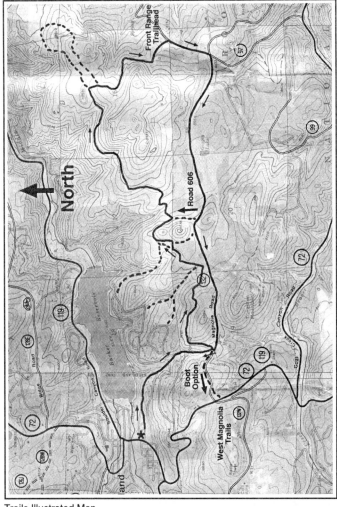

Trails Illustrated Map

DISTANCE: 12.6 miles

PHYSICAL: ☺☺☾

TECHNICAL: ☺☺

TERRAIN: Firm to loose trail with ruts; sand and gravel; a few rocks

GAIN: 2,400 feet

MAP: Trails Illustrated - Deckers/Rampart Range

This is a grunt of a ride with a continuous 5+ mile climb without relief. On the positive side, you are not likely to have much bike traffic and the descent back to the start is simply a hoot. Portions of the trail still show the ravages of the 1996 Buffalo Creek fire and hence there may be sections of sand, gravel and ruts to contend with. But with much of the trail seeing recent maintenance, rerouting, and a new bridge across the South Platte, the climb is now much more biker friendly than in the past.

ACCESS: Drive west on U.S. 285 just past Conifer to Foxton Road. Head south on Foxton Road all the way down to the North Fork of the South Platte. Turn left and drive along the river. After crossing over the South Platte River, continue for about half a mile to a foot bridge over the main stem of the South Platte and a Colorado Trail trailhead parking area complete with restroom.

DESCRIPTION: Cross the foot bridge and turn left following the river for a short distance before beginning an extended climb with many switchbacks. The trails reaches the nose of a ridge **(0.9)** then passes an old mine as the trail now enters the fire area providing some dramatic views of the surrounding area. After a short drop the trail keeps climbing to the northwest. Just after crossing a wash **(2.6)**, reenter the thin forest where the trail surface becomes much smoother and more enjoyable. Keep plugging as the trail keeps climbing, but now with a few short drops that breaks up the grind and now with denser forest. After a series of switchbacks, a good view point **(5.3)** and the high point of the ride is encountered. You have climbed about 1,800 feet to this point. Drop from the view point for half a mile before the final climb to Forest Road 538 **(6.3)**. Turnaround here, smile and take satisfaction on how few mountain bikers you encountered on your way up and how few you likely will pass on the fast descent.

TRAIL OPTION: One can press on along the Colorado Trail to the paved Jeffco 126 which lies 4+ miles beyond. There is some climbing to get to pavement, but the trail generally rolls towards the south with many short ups and downs.

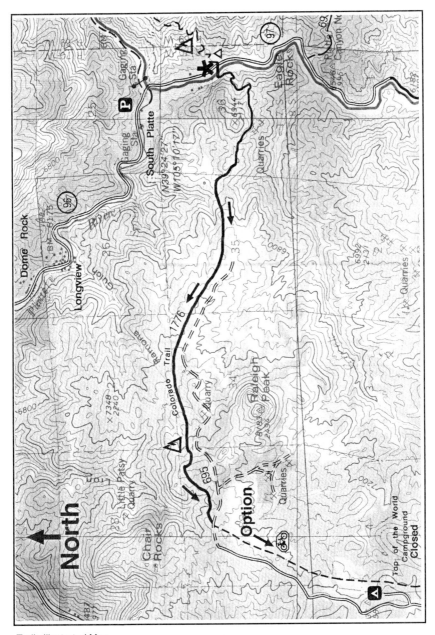

Trails Illustrated Map

RIDE 4 DELL GULCH

DISTANCE: 9.6 miles

PHYSICAL: ○

TECHNICAL: ○

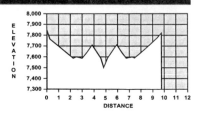

TERRAIN: Smooth forest road; two-track trail

GAIN: 1,070 feet

MAP: Trails Illustrated - Deckers/Rampart Range

Not exactly single track on this ride, but this closed forest road makes for an easy ride as this well groomed road is beginning to grow back to a trail. In a few years, this road will be double or single-track trail. Smooth, gravelly turf is the word that best describes this out-and-back ride. Due to the Buffalo Creek fire of 1996, motorized Trail 695 has been closed, so this is a much more peaceful ride than in the past, although 695 had some nice sections of single track. There may be a day use fee so bring some dollars.

ACCESS: On US 285, drive west to Pine Junction and turn left on Jefferson County 126. Drive 13.2 miles through both Pine Grove and Buffalo Creek to Forest Road 550. Turn right on to 550 and find the trailhead 0.1 miles from Jefferson County 126 on your right.

DESCRIPTION: Head back to Jefferson County 126 and turn left on the pavement. Drop on the road a short distance and turn right at the first gated road on your right **(0.2)**. Pass through the gate, now on FR 530 and spiral your way generally downhill for several miles. At the "Trail Closed" sign **(3.0)**, (Trail 695) the road curves left and climbs/rolls a bit. At an abandoned piece of construction equipment **(3.7)**, the road dives one more time down to its end **(4.8)**. While bikes, horses, and hikers are allowed beyond this end point, the USFS has dropped numerous logs across the trail making it unridable down to Spring Creek. Now for the hard part, reverse course and pedal, ugh, back up the hill to the start.

TRAIL OPTION: This ride can be combined with the Colorado Trail to add more miles to your trip. After completing Dell Gulch, bike a short distance north along Jefferson County 126 to hook up with the Colorado Trail which will be on your right. Head northeasterly along the Colorado Trail to Chair Rocks on this intermediate singletrack trail.

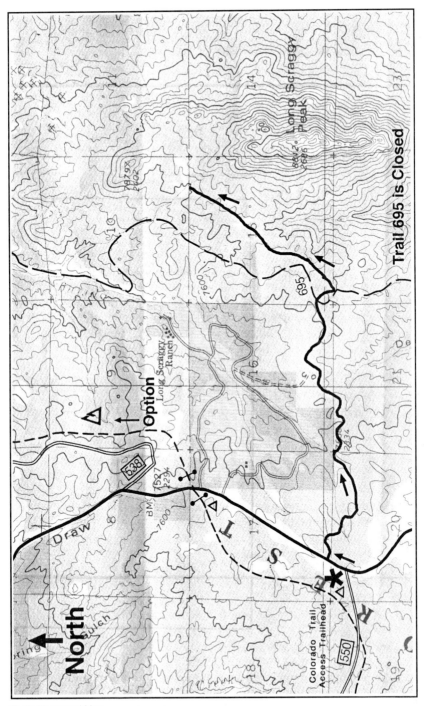

Trails Illustrated Map

RIDE 5 FIVE PARKS

DISTANCE: 22.5 miles

PHYSICAL: ✿✿✿

TECHNICAL: ✿✿

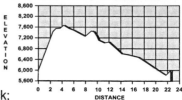

TERRAIN: Every type of single track; pavement and dirt roads

GAIN: 3,450 feet

MAP: USGS - Evergreen and Morrison

This ride strings together 5 parks; Mt. Falcon, Pence, O'Fallon, Corwina, and Lair O' the Bear. This string of parks makes for one of the better longer, challenging, close-in rides along the Front Range. Most of the climbing is done early on Mt. Falcon, but every park has some climbing that adds to the total elevation gain. The descent starting from Pence Park is frequently fast and exciting, while Lair O' The Bear Park provides a nice mellow finish for your single track experience.

ACCESS: On U.S. 285, travel west from Denver and exit on Colorado 8. Travel north towards Morrison for 1.3 miles and turn left on Forest Avenue. Follow the signs to the Mt. Falcon trailhead.

DESCRIPTION: Crank up the Castle Trail to the Meadow Trail which is directly across from Walker's Home Ruin **(3.1)**. Turn left on Meadow Trail and descend at first, before climbing to Old Ute **(3.4)**. Turn left and climb a short distance before turning left again on Old Ute. Follow Old Ute around to Devil's Elbow **(3.7)** and turn left, plunging down on Devil's Elbow. Take the left fork on the loop and complete the Devil's Elbow loop. Drop back to Meadow Trail intersection and continue straight and uphill on Meadow Trail and find your way to the west parking lot. Take the Mount Falcon Road down to Picutis road. Turn right on Picutis and continue down to Parmalee Gulch Road **(8.0)**. Turn right and climb on Parmalee Road for 1.0 mile to Inca Rd. **(9.0)**. Pass the Pence Park parking lot and spy the Bear Creek Trail on your right just as you start to descend on the road. Follow the trail uphill where it cross a ridge and descends to a dirt road. Take dirt the road and swing around to the other side of the gulch and descend to a spot with three trail splits. **(10.2)**. Go left (north) on the middle split and continue descending to another trail split **(10.7)**. Take the right split and start a short climb. Stay on the well defined Bear Creek Trail as it loops and rolls through the pines and crosses many lesser defined splinter trails. After completing a long climb, find yourself near a small white rock out cropping **(12.8)** with a good view of the valley. Quickly descend towards the north and ultimately Bear Creek.

Turn right at Bear Creek and follow it downstream on superb trail now within Lair O' The Bear Park. Turn right at Dipper Bridge **(15.4)**, then right on Bruin Bluff Trail and begin climbing once again. After zigzagging on some fun switchbacks, drop back to the creek and continue on Bruin Bluff Trail until you finally come out at a parking lot **(17.1)**. Find State Hwy 74, turn right and pedal into Morrison **(22.0)**. In Morrison, turn right at the first signal, Colorado 8, and bike uphill back to the Mt. Falcon trailhead.

TRAIL OPTIONS: A. The ride can be done in the opposite direction, but you will encounter many more riders/hikers on the Mt. Falcon descent. **B.** Some riders like to start in downtown Morrison and avoid the crowded Mt. Falcon parking lot.

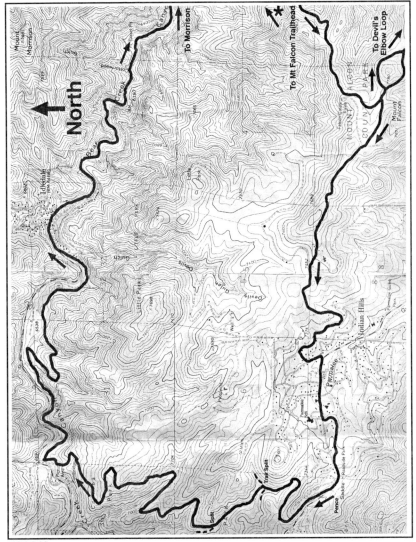

RIDE 6 FLYING J

DISTANCE: 4.0 miles

PHYSICAL: ⭕

TECHNICAL: ⭕◖

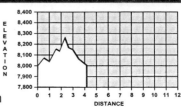

TERRAIN: Smooth single track with occasional rocks

GAIN: 360 feet

MAP: USGS - Conifer

This heavily forested, short, and relatively flat ride is a great beginner trail. This recent addition to the Jeffco Open Space system has just enough technical sections to keep things varied and just enough up and down to keep one huff'n. Consider doing laps on the Shadow Pine Trail to add miles, reversing the direction to keep things interesting. In the winter, this makes for a nice beginner cross country ski loop.

ACCESS: Drive west on US 285 to Conifer and exit on Colorado 73. Head north towards Evergreen for about 1.3 miles to Shadow Mountain Drive where the small trailhead can be seen adjacent to Colorado 73. There is a second, larger trailhead complete with restrooms and picnic facilities a bit farther north on Colorado 73. Look for the sign.

DESCRIPTION: Jump on the Junction House Trail and quickly cross a bridge over a wetlands and climb to the Shadow Pine Trail **(0.6)**. Either direction along Shadow Pine makes a fine ride, but continue counter clockwise along the Shadow Pine Trail. Cross a service road and pass adjacent to the second trailhead along your way to a small creek **(1.2)** all the time continuing to climb. There are tightly spaced trees along the way to keep things interesting. Near mile two, a switchback takes you to the high point of the ride **(2.3)** where the trail begins a rolling descent again through tightly spaced trees. Cross two access roads before finding yourself all too soon back at the Junction House Trail **(3.5)**. Turn right on Junction House and pedal on back to the start.

TRAIL OPTION: With limited parking at the southern trailhead, consider either parking at the northern trailhead or biking to the park from Conifer.

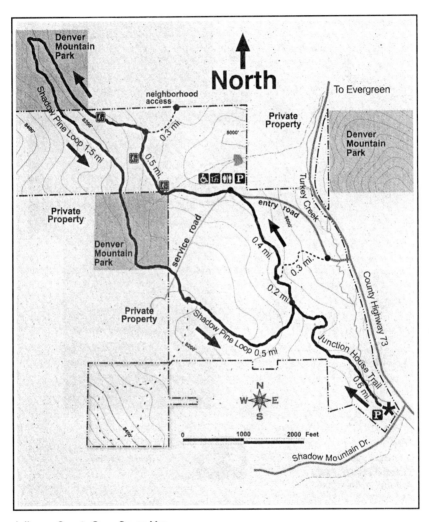

Jefferson County Open Space Map

DISTANCE: 23.0 miles

PHYSICAL: ○○○

TECHNICAL: ○○

TERRAIN: Smooth to rutted hardpack; frequent rocks and roots

GAIN: 4,000 feet

MAP: Trail TopoGraphics Map - Kenosha

This out and back ride along the Colorado Trail is a well known, popular high altitude excursion, especially when the aspens are turning. And what a great view from the top of Georgia Pass and what a fast drop back into Jefferson Creek. The final climb on the way back can be a killer for those not accustom to high altitude riding and relatively high elevation gain. Dress warmly since it gets cold at 11,800 feet, even in the height of summer.

ACCESS: Drive west on US 285 through Grant to the top of Kenosha Pass. Park on the right, just outside of the campground entrance. Restrooms and additional parking can be found on the left side of the road.

DESCRIPTION: Jump on the Colorado Trail, swing around the campground and begin climbing to a ridge **(1.0).** From the ridge, start a fun descent frequently in the aspens and with nice views of South Park to Guernsey Creek **(3.0).** The trail begins a slow climb to the north of the rocky Jefferson Hill with a crossing of Deadman's creek along the way. Pass through a cattle gate **(5.3)** before dropping to Jefferson Lake Road. Cross the road and Jefferson Creek **(6.7)** and begin the final, long assault - it is a long steady grind up to the pass. Where the trail makes a loop back to the west, a fine view point is encountered and a lunch stop should be considered. As you reach tree line, spot a cairn where a distinct trail takes off the to right **(11.9).** This is the Trail 643, West Jefferson, which is the return option. Keep heading up as the last half mile gets steeper and finally reaches Georgia Pass and the Continental Divide. **(12.5).** After enjoying the view return via the same route.

TRAIL OPTIONS: A. Trail 643 takes off half mile from the summit of Georgia Pass and heads northeast before dropping south into the Jefferson Creek drainage and ultimately back to the Colorado Trail. It is a nice fun alternative with fewer riders likely to be encounter. **B.** Yes you can drop all the way into Breckenridge. Many riders use a shuttle to return to Kenosha Pass.

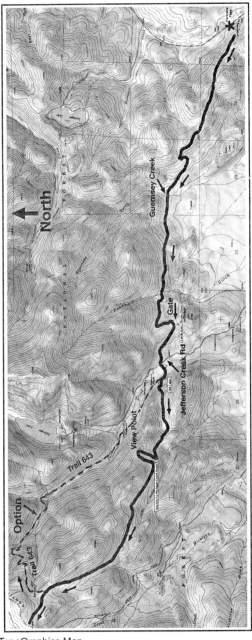

Trail TopoGraphics Map   *Page - 27*

RIDE 8 GOLDEN GATE WEST

DISTANCE: 10.5 miles

PHYSICAL: ⟡⟡⟡

TECHNICAL: ⟡⟡⟡

TERRAIN: Narrow to wide single track; some loose rocks and gravel

GAIN: 2,000 feet

MAPS: Golden Gate State Park

This ride strings together several trails to form a nice loop on the west side of the park. While the majority of this ride is technically easy there are several rocky climbs where one might be force to walk. If you want a more technical downhill experience, do this ride in the opposite direction. This ride has been closed to mountain bikers in the past, so please be courtesy and watch for the many horses you may encounter along the loop.

ACCESS: From Golden, take Highway 93 north to Golden Gate Canyon Road. Turn left and continue for 12.3 miles to the park. Continue past the Visitors Center (after getting your park pass) and turn right at the trailhead sign just past Kriley Pond. Climb to the parking lot above Kriley Pond.

DESCRIPTION: Start climbing on the Blue Goose Trail and quickly find the Mule Deer Trail **(0.7).** Turn right on Mule Deer and after gutting through a tough, steep rocky section of the trail, it becomes smoother and flatter to the intersection with the Black Bear Trail **(1.2).** Staying on the Mule Deer Trail, pass a cabin on your way up to a ridge. Descend off the ridge, passing the Snow Shoe Trail twice along the way and then climb again staying on Mule Deer Trail. After the trail makes a hard left **(3.5)** climb a frustrating hill and bounce your way along to the Gap Road **(4.9).** Cross the road and turn right on the Raccoon Trail where a fun descent is now had. After crossing a bridge **(6.0),** the trail veers left towards the campground and climbs back to the Gap Road **(6.7)** passing several trail splits along the way and coming the Elk Trail. Now begin a frequently fast drop, sometimes in the trees, sometimes in meadows. After passing the Ole' Barn Trailhead **(8.7),** the trail becomes Mule Deer Trail again and drops to the Mtn. Base Road. Cross the road and climb back to Blue Grouse Trail **(9.8).** Turn right and descend back to the start.

TRAIL OPTION: For a really long day, string this ride and the Mountain Lion/Snow Shoe Trails on the east side of the park together for a figure-8 loop.

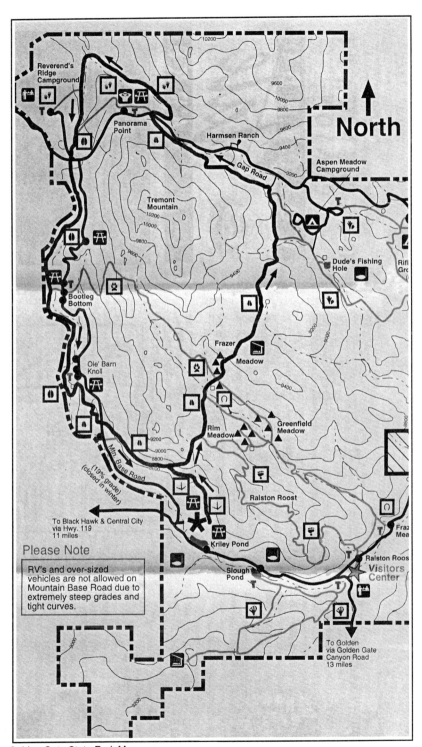

North

Reverend's Ridge Campground

Panorama Point

Harmsen Ranch

Gap Road

Aspen Meadow Campground

Tremont Mountain

Dude's Fishing Hole

Rifl Gro

Bootleg Bottom

Frazer Meadow

Ole' Barn Knoll

Rim Meadow

Greenfield Meadow

Ralston Roost

Mtn. Base Road
(19% grade)
(closed in winter)

To Black Hawk & Central City
via Hwy. 119
11 miles

Kriley Pond

Slough Pond

Fraz
Mea

Ralston Roos
Visitors
Center

Please Note

RV's and over-sized
vehicles are not allowed on
Mountain Base Road due to
extremely steep grades and
tight curves.

To Golden
via Golden Gate
Canyon Road
13 miles

RIDE 9 HEIL RANCH

DISTANCE: 7.6 miles

PHYSICAL: ◐◖

TECHNICAL: ○

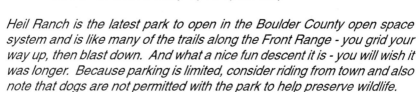

TERRAIN: Smooth and wide with a few rocks; short section of dirt road

GAIN: 1,000 feet

MAP: Boulder County Open Space Map

Heil Ranch is the latest park to open in the Boulder County open space system and is like many of the trails along the Front Range - you grid your way up, then blast down. And what a nice fun descent it is - you will wish it was longer. Because parking is limited, consider riding from town and also note that dogs are not permitted with the park to help preserve wildlife.

ACCESS: From Broadway and US 36 on the north side of Boulder, drive north on US 36 for 4.7 miles to Lefthand Canyon Road. Turn left and travel just over a mile to Geer Canyon Road. Turn right on Geer Canyon and drive another 1.5 miles to the trailhead.

DESCRIPTION: Near the north end of the parking lot, pickup the wide road-like Wapiti Trail and climb for half a mile where the trail turns left and becomes single track. Begin a steady climb on relatively smooth trail. After crossing an access road **(1.3)** and swinging by an old foundation, find yourself at the Ponderosa Loop **(2.5)**. Either direction is fun, but turn left and climb a short distance where the trail turns right and begins a gentle downhill. After crossing a fire road, find an overlook with great views of Hall Ranch to the north. Continue on the loop and after passing an interesting rock wall, climb back to the Wapiti Trail **(5.1)**. Consider turning around and doing the loop in the other direction to add a couple of more miles. But if not, turn left and blast down keeping one's speed in check back to the start and all too quickly the end of the ride.

TRAIL OPTIONS: If you are inclined to bike to Heil Ranch from Boulder, take Lee Hill Road to Old Stage Coach Road which will drop to Lefthand Road. Turn right on Lefthand Road and crank to Geer Canyon Road turning left towards the park. Coming soon is the much awaited connector trail over to Hall Ranch as well as a new loop trail within Heil Ranch. Watch for them in the near future.

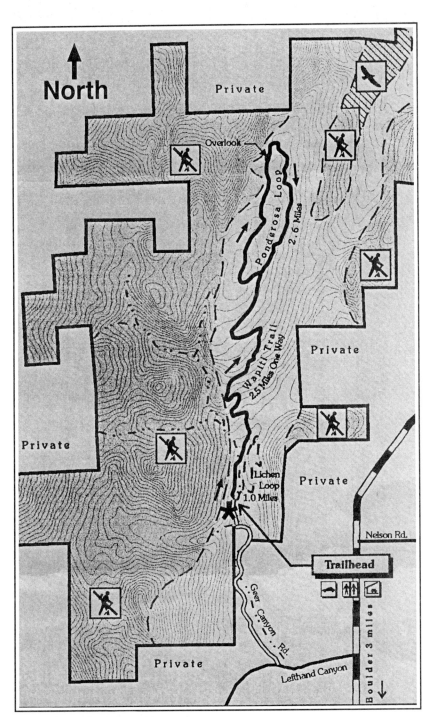

North

Private

Overlook

Ponderosa Loop
2.6 Miles

Private

Wapiti Trail
2.5 Miles One Way

Private

Private

Lichen
Loop
1.0 Miles

Nelson Rd.

Private

Trailhead

Geer Canyon Rd.

Boulder 3 miles

Private

Lefthand Canyon

RIDE 10 INDIAN CREEK LOOP

DISTANCE: 14.6 miles

PHYSICAL: ⚙⚙⚙

TECHNICAL: ⚙⚙⚙

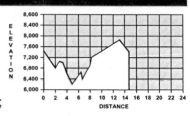

TERRAIN: Firm to loose hardpack; log ramps and roots

GAIN: 2,500 feet

MAP: Trails Illustrated - Deckers/Rampart Range

This loop trail is the product of equestrians and mountain bikers coming together to build a multiuse, primitive trail. While not terribly rocky or technical, there are some very steep, long climbs where you may walk. There are also some fun log ramps along the way to play on. The trail can be done in either direction with equal fun and climbing pain. The clockwise route as described puts a downhill at the end, while counter clockwise will put a most of the climbing at the end. Your pick - either way is a blast..

ACCESS: Drive South on US 85 (Santa Fe Drive) to Sedalia and turn right on Colorado 67. Follow Colorado 67 for about 10 miles to the Indian Creek Campground, just past Rampart Range Road. Turn right and park near the restroom. There may be a day use fee so bring some dollars.

DESCRIPTION: Note that the trail number is 800, you'll be following signs with this number for the entire loop. Head west, down the gravel road, through the equestrian campground and find the start of the single track at the end of the campground. The trail descents along Bear Creek, crossing it twice before a short climb to a 3-way intersection **(2.4)**. Turn left and keep climbing to the ridge where the trail rolls along. A quick descent from the ridge brings one to the Roxborough Loop. Turn right and follow it to a "T" intersection **(6.0)**. Turn right and climb towards the State Park. This portion of the trail starts steeply, but is short as you drop to Mill Creek and a large meadow. The trail turns south and then climbs to a powerline and a 4-way intersection **(7.2)**. Turn right and continue south, generally climbing, but with some short, fun descents to mix it up. One finally pops out under a powerline tower and dirt road **(9.9)** after a long climb in the pines. Turn left and follow the main road as it winds its way south and gains elevation. Pass through a four-way road split **(12.3)** staying on the main road. Spot a faint single track **(13.0)** that takes off through the oaks on your right and begin descending back to the trailhead.

TRAIL OPTION: If you access this loop via Waterton Canyon Trailhead, consider doing the loop in the opposite, counter clockwise direction. This puts the climb up to the campground early and the single track decent at the end. Total mileage is about 28 with well over 3,400 feet of vertical gain.

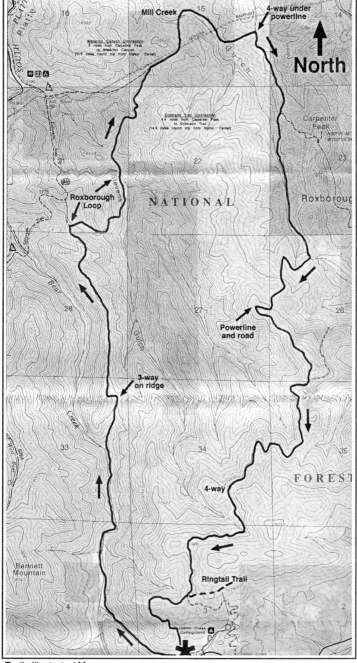

RIDE 11 LAIR O' THE BEAR

DISTANCE: 2.0 miles

PHYSICAL: ○

TECHNICAL: ○

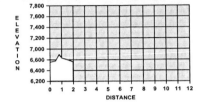

TERRAIN: Smooth hardpack

GAIN: 160 feet

MAP: Jefferson County Open Space - Lair O' The Bear

OK, so I had to put an easy, short ride in the book. Lair O' The Bear was chosen because it is close to Denver and because it can be a good late season idyllic ride when other trails are snow covered. Try laps, if you need to do more then stretch your legs or checkout the new Bear Creek Trail which takes off to Pence Park at the west end of the Lair O' The Bear.

ACCESS: From C470, exit at Morrison and travel west on Colorado 74 through Morrison and Idledale for approximately six miles to the park entrance.

DESCRIPTION: Find the Brittlefern Trail on the north side of the parking lot and begin pedaling east on the wide, gravel trail. The trail quickly crosses the entrance road to the park and then Bear Creek **(0.2)**. Just after crossing the creek, the trail turns west becoming the Bruin Bluff Trail and begins a steady climb on the mostly rock-less trail. Two short switchbacks put you at the high point for the ride **(0.9)**, where the trail then begins a fun, curvy descend back to the creek. Cross over Bear Creek on Dipper Bridge and turn right back to the parking area **(2.0)**. Seriously consider the trail options to explore more of the park.

TRAIL OPTIONS: A. A trail now extends the length of the park along Bear Creek in both directions from the parking area. From the parking lot, go west (upstream), staying along the creek for just over one mile until the obvious end of the trail and gate. Going east (downstream) is shorter, ending at Little Park 0.7 miles from the parking lot. Combining the basic ride with these two easy options makes for a nice trail combo. **B.** There is now an additional single track connection called the Bear Creek Trail from Lair O' The Bear to Pence Park. This stellar trail can be found at the west end of the park (see Pence to Lair ride number 16). The climb out of Bear Creek on the Bear Creek Trail is stiff and definitely not a beginner ride.

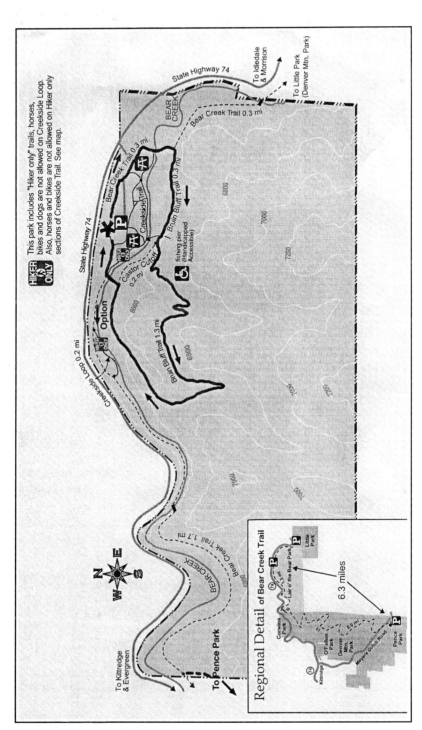

This park includes "Hiker only" trails, horses, bikes and dogs are not allowed on Creekside Loop. Also, horses and bikes are not allowed on Hiker only sections of Creekside Trail. See map.

HIKER ONLY

State Highway 74

To Idledale & Morrison

To Little Park (Denver Mtn. Park)

State Highway 74

BEAR CREEK

Bear Creek Trail 0.3 mi

Bear Creek Trail 0.3 mi

Creekside Trail

Bruin Bluff Trail 0.3 mi

6800

7000

7200

fishing pier (Handicapped Accessible)

Castor Cutoff 0.2 mi

6800

Bruin Bluff Trail 1.3 mi

6800

Creekside Loop 0.2 mi

Option

6800

7000

7000

7200

N E W S

7000

7000

BEAR CREEK

Bear Creek Trail 1.7 mi

To Kittredge & Evergreen

To Pence Park

Regional Detail of Bear Creek Trail

Little Park

74

Lair o' the Bear Park

1.3 mi

6.3 miles

Conwina Park

O'Fallon Park

Denver Mtn. Park

6.0 mi

Meyers Gulch Road

Pence Park

74

Kittridge

DISTANCE: 16.2 miles

PHYSICAL: ⚙⚙

TECHNICAL: ⚙⚙

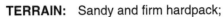

TERRAIN: Sandy and firm hardpack; occasional root or rock; forest road

GAIN: 1,700 feet

MAPS: Trails Illustrated - Deckers/Rampart Range

This ride combines two of the lesser used trails in the Buffalo Creek trail system, Tramway and Lower Gashouse, with closed Forest Road and a section of the Colorado Trail for a nice easy single track experience. I like this ride because you will have more solitude and see fewer riders. Sections of this ride can be a wee bit sandy or gravelly so be careful.

ACCESS: Drive west on U.S. 285 past Conifer to Pine Junction. Turn left at the signal (Jefferson County 126) and drive just over 12 miles to the hamlet of Buffalo Creek, passing through Pine Grove along the way. Park in an area just south of the USFS Work Station, on your left, just after you cross the creek and enter town.

DESCRIPTION: Hop back on the pavement heading north and quickly turn left onto Buffalo Creek Road (FR 543) just after crossing Buffalo Creek. Gradually climb on this dirt road, first passing Sandy Wash and then Baldy/ Gashouse **(4.4)** trails. Less than half a mile from the Baldy Trail, spot Tramway on your left. Take Tramway and steadily climb to the Colorado Trail **(6.2)** crossing FR 550 along the way. Turn right on the Colorado Trail, pass the Green Mountain Trail and descent to the main campground road within the Meadows Group Campground **(8.5)**. Turn right and drop to FR 550. Turn left on FR 550, pass FR 543 and climb to the Gashouse Gulch road turnoff **(9.5)**. Climb to the end of the road and a log fence. Find and take the single track to the right of the fence and gently climb a short distance to a forest burn area. As you enter the edge of the fire area, the trail begins to drop with lots of gravel, sand and ruts to contend with. Drop to the confluence with the Baldy Trail **(11.6)** and then quickly back to FR 543 **(11.8)**. Turn left on FR 543 and cruise back to Buffalo Creek.

TRAIL OPTION: Of course, with all of the wonderful trails in the Buffalo Creek system, one can think of many different combinations of loops. Add Baldy? Add Green Mountain? Add?

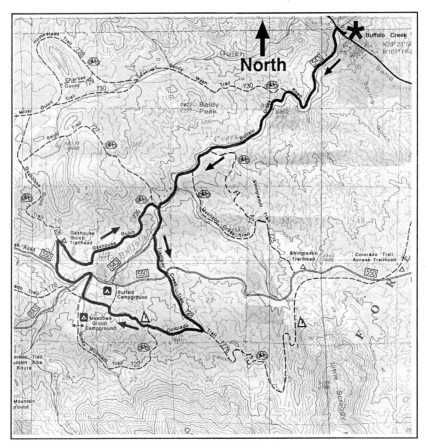

Trails Illustrated Map

DISTANCE: 4.3 miles

PHYSICAL: ⚙

TECHNICAL: ⚙☾

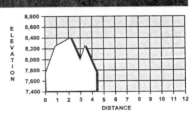

TERRAIN: Smooth and rocky hardpack

GAIN: 1,000 feet

MAP: Trail TopoGraphics - Maxwell Falls

While not the longest ride in the world, this ride has a challenging, rocky climb to start and a fair amount of climbing for the short distance. It also has some easy smooth trail. This is also a popular dog walk and hiking trail so you may encounter a lot of pedestrian traffic, both two and four legged.

ACCESS: On U.S. 285, travel west from Denver and turn right on Hwy 73 in Conifer and head towards Evergreen. After 3.1 miles, turn left on to Blue Creek Road. When Blue Creek Road ends, turn left on Brook Forest Road and travel just over one mile to the trailhead which is on your left.

DESCRIPTION: Start climbing immediately towards the upper parking lot and quickly encounter the rocky portion of the ride. The rocks are firmly planted with good lines to weave your way around/over the rocks. After crossing a small brook, climb to an open area with many small pine trees and a 4-way trail intersection **(0.9)**. Turn left on the wider trail and climb a short distance before rolling to a creek. Pass through the creek veering left and crank up to the upper parking area **(2.1)**. Reverse course and drop back towards the creek, but veer left on the obvious trail towards the falls just before recrossing the creek. Pass the Cliff Loop trail and shortly find yourself at Maxwell Falls **(2.5)**. Switchback your way down to the creek and follow the creek downstream to a bridge **(3.0)**. A spur on your left just before the bridge dead ends at private property, in case you had any ideas. From the bridge climb steadily back to the 4-way **(3.4)**, and then back through the rocky trail section back to the start.

TRAIL OPTIONS: A. At the 4-way trail junction at mile 0.9, one can go right to add more mileage. Go right, uphill, and do a short rocky loop that brings one back to the 4-way. It will add less than a mile to the total ride. **B.** One can access the Cub Creek Trail from the upper parking lot/picnic grounds. To reach Cub Creek, hop on the pavement turning right and pedal a short distance until you see the turnoff sign. The Cub Creek Trail is a tough, frequently rocky SOB and not for the faint of heart.

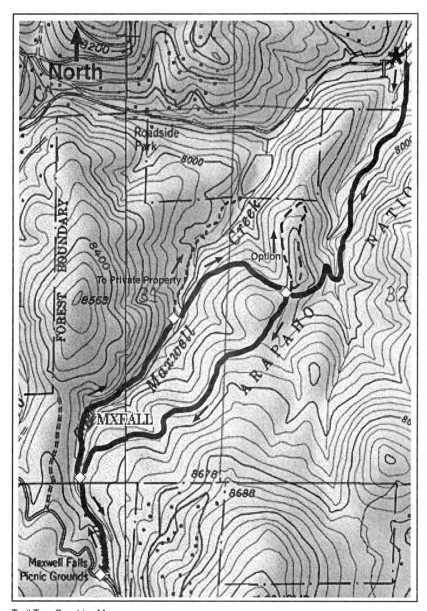

Trail TopoGraphics Map

DISTANCE: 4.7 miles

PHYSICAL: ◑◐

TECHNICAL: ◑◐

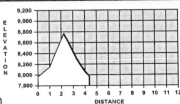

TERRAIN: Smooth single track with waterbars; occasional easy rocky sections

GAIN: 900 feet

MAP: Jefferson County Open Space - Meyers Ranch

Typical of many Jeffco Parks, up you go with a quick fly back down. This short ride is generally smooth yet has a couple of challenging waterbars and rocks to navigate. It is a steady climb with a fair amount of elevation gain. A quick evening ride or a ride to introduce a beginner to the pleasure of single track is in store with this park. This north facing park holds its snow well so wait until it dries for the best riding.

ACCESS: On US 285, head west towards Conifer and watch for the sign. The park is about one mile before Conifer and just before Aspen Park.

DESCRIPTION: Start climbing on the wide road to the restrooms where the single track begins and veer right on Owl's Perch Trail. Climb on Owl's Perch to Lodge Pole Loop **(0.6)** and turn right. The Lodge Pole Loop is fairly flat to start but steadily climbs to Sunny Aspen Trail **(1.2)**. Turn right on Sunny Aspen and climb to the shelter encountering several waterbars along the way **(1.5)**. Turn right on Old Ski Run Trail and steadily climb, now with more rocks to challenge you. At the loop portion of Old Ski Run **(2.2)**, continue straight (clockwise) and continue climbing. After completing the loop, head back down to the shelter and turn right on Sunny Aspen Trail **(3.5)**. Drop to Lodge Pole Loop **(4.0)** and turn right after encountering several tight switchbacks. Continue down through the picnic area and back to the start. There may be considerable foot traffic in the lower section of the park so keep your speed down.

TRAIL OPTIONS: A. After completing the Old Ski Run Trail loop on top, reverse and do the trail the other way. **B.** One can also double back on Lodge Pole Loop **(4.0)** near the bottom by going left instead of right. This will add just under one additional mile of trail.

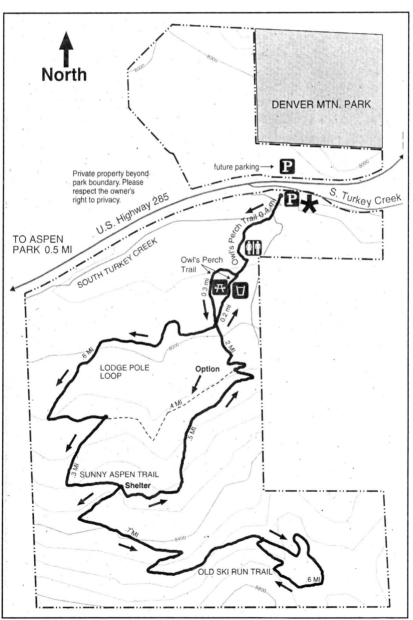

North

DENVER MTN. PARK

Private property beyond park boundary. Please respect the owner's right to privacy.

future parking →

U.S. Highway 285

S. Turkey Creek

Owl's Perch Trail 0.4 mi

TO ASPEN PARK 0.5 MI

SOUTH TURKEY CREEK

Owl's Perch Trail

0.3 mi

0.2 mi

.2 mi

.6 MI

LODGE POLE LOOP

Option

.4 MI

.5 MI

.3 MI

SUNNY ASPEN TRAIL

Shelter

.7 MI

OLD SKI RUN TRAIL

.6 MI

RIDE 15 MORRISON CREEK

DISTANCE: 17.0 miles

PHYSICAL: ○○

TECHNICAL: ○(

TERRAIN: Sandy and firm hardpack; occasional root or rock; forest road

GAIN: 1,690 feet

MAPS: Trails Illustrated - Deckers/Rampart Range

The recently reopened Morrison Creek Trail adds yet another trail in the Buffalo Creek trail system. The Morrison Creek Trail was closed due to the Buffalo Creek fire and the destruction of the forest can still be seen. This lesser used connector trail between the heavily biked Colorado Trail and FR 543 expands one's biking options and gives the rider many loop options.

ACCESS: Drive west on U.S. 285 past Conifer to Pine Junction. Turn left at the signal (Jefferson County 126) and drive just over 12 miles to the hamlet of Buffalo Creek. Park in an area just south of the USFS Work Station, on your left, just after you cross the creek and enter town.

DESCRIPTION: Hop back on the pavement heading north and quickly turn left onto Buffalo Creek Road (FR 543) just after crossing Buffalo Creek. Gently climb on this dirt road, first passing Sandy Wash and the Baldy/Gashouse **(4.4)** trails. Less than half a mile from the Baldy trail, spot Tramway on your left. Take Tramway and steadily climb to the Colorado Trail **(6.2)** crossing FR 550 along the way. Turn left on the Colorado Trail and begin a mile long ascent to a high point. Begin a series of short drops and climbs as you head east along the Colorado Trail. After crossing a small brook with a stone bridge, climb to the top of a ridge and spot a single track on your left **(9.9)**. Take this trail, the Morrison Creek/Shinglemill Trail, and quickly drop to FR 550. Cross the road and soon enter the burn area. Glide down through the burn area and interesting rock formations until you join up with the Morrison Creek Trail. Take Morrison Creek Trail downhill, following the creek until you arrive at FR 543 **(13.7)**. Turn right and cruise on back to the start.

TRAIL OPTIONS: A. The ride can be done in the opposite direction which gives the rider a fun drop on Tramway Trail. However, the climb on Morrison Creek/Shinglemill can be fairly sandy, loose and has plenty of gravel which makes for tough climbing in many spots. Still a good ride. **B.** On your next outing take Shinglemill Trail downhill to FR 543 instead of Morrison Creek.

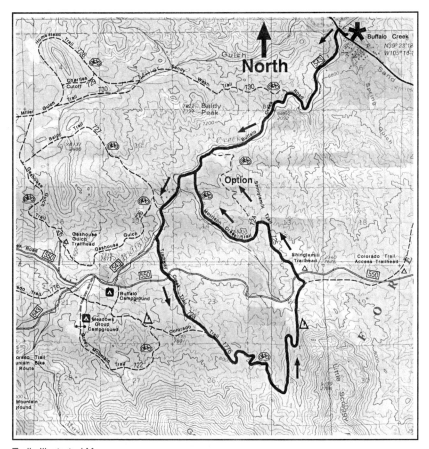

Trails Illustrated Map

RIDE 16 PENCE TO LAIR

DISTANCE: 10.2 miles

PHYSICAL: ○○

TECHNICAL: ○(

TERRAIN: Firm hardpack;
a few rocks

GAIN: 2,250 feet

MAP: USGS - Evergreen

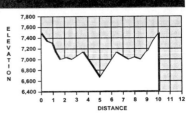

This new corridor trail, Bear Creek Trail, provides access into several different foothill parks - one now has more ride alternatives in the Evergreen area. The trail is typical trail construction found along the Front Range - reasonably wide, well planned, and frequently fast. The final drop into Lair O' The Bear Park is fun and sometimes technical, but a stiff climb out of Bear Creek is in store on the return. Some novice riders may want to avoid the final descent and turn around at the white rocks overlook.

ACCESS: *From C-470, exit at Morrison and head west following Bear Creek passing Lair O' The Bear Park along the way. In Kittredge, turn left on Myers Gulch Road (head towards Mount Falcon) and drive up a long hill. As you crest the hill, find the Pence Park parking lot on your right.*

DESCRIPTION: Find the Bear Creek Trail on the north side of the parking lot and take it across Myers Gulch Road. Follow the trail uphill where it cross a ridge and descends to a wide dirt road. Turn right on the dirt road and swing around to the other side of the gulch and descend to a spot where three trails/roads intersect **(1.2)**. Go left (north) on the narrow middle split and continue descending to where a narrow trail comes in on your left and below you **(1.7)**. Veer right on the wider trail and start a short climb. Stay on this well defined main trail as it loops and rolls through the pines and crosses many lesser defined splinter trails/roads. After crossing a small drainage **(3.1)** begin an extended climb that has several nice views of Mt. Evans off to the west. After completing this long climb, find yourself near a small white rock outcropping **(3.6)** with a good view of the Bear Creek valley below. Start a fun, steep, and sometimes technical descent towards the north and into the Bear Creek drainage **(5.1)** . After considering the trail option, turn around and head back the way you came.

TRAIL OPTION: To add 4.5 easy miles, do the trails within Lair O' The Bear Park (See Ride 11). Head east along the creek then do the Bruin Bluff/Brittlefern loop.

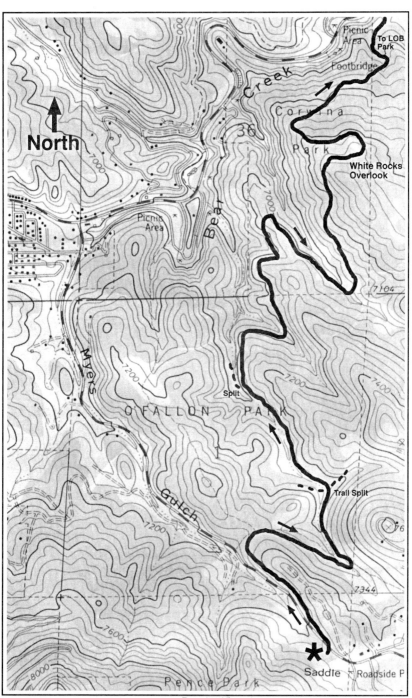

North

To LOB Park

Picnic Area

Footbridge

Creek

Corwina Park

White Rocks Overlook

36

7000

Bear

Picnic Area

7104

7200

O'FALLON PARK

7200

7400

Split

Myers

Trail Split

Gulch

7200

76

7344

7600

Saddle Roadside P

Pence Park

8000

DISTANCE: 19.2 miles

PHYSICAL: ⚙⚙⚙

TECHNICAL: ⚙⚙

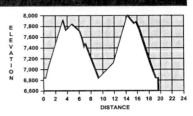

TERRAIN: Smooth and sandy hardpack; forest road

GAIN: 2,600 feet

MAP: Trails Illustrated - Deckers/Rampart Range

The loop ride really only has two "hills" to climb, both of which are long and extended. And of course, there are two long stellar downhills. The best part of this ride is Charlie's Cutoff which snakes it's way over and around slick rock. Charlie's is an absolute kick and something of a rarity around Denver. Strawberry Jack Trail has been relocated/rebuild in several sections and there is much more gravel and sand than in the past. Most of the ride is through partially to complete forest burn areas.

ACCESS: On US. 285, drive to Pine Junction and turn left on Jefferson County 126 for 5.7 miles to Pine Valley Ranch. Turn right at the park entrance sign and follow the signs to the parking lot.

DESCRIPTION: Find the Narrow Gauge Trail on the north side of the river and head upstream to the North Fork View Trail **(0.3)** turning left on to it. Cross the river and pick up the Buck Gulch Trail and begin climbing on the wide, road-like trail. The trail switchbacks to the right **(0.8)** after passing the Strawberry Jack Trail and steepens on loose gravel. The trail climbs steadily on this loose surface to the junction with the Skipper Trail, just as you meet Forest Road 552 **(3.2).** Turn left and fly down on the frequently sandy and rutted Skipper Trail before climbing out of Buck Gulch to a four-way intersection **(4.5).** Turn right and continue climbing. At the crest of the next hill, find Charlie's Cutoff **(5.1)** on your left and take it as you generally drop to the Homestead Trail riding some cool slickrock along the way. Turn right on Homestead and continue downhill. Just as you pop out next to a large meadow, the trail veers left and now becomes the Sandy Wash Trail **(6.9).** Follow Sandy Wash to a stream crossing then a quick climb into a burn area. Sandy Wash Trail soon starts a long drop to Buffalo Creek. As you spy the road below and as Sandy Wash Trail veers left, take the short spur down to Forest Road 543 **(9.8).** As an option, you can continue to take Sandy Wash for about one mile as the trail parallels the road and ultimately unites with Forest Road 543. Turn right on the road and now start the second long climb to the marked Baldy/Gashouse Trail sign **(12.5).**

Climb a short distance and turn right on the Baldy Trail and climb to a ridge, but not before finding yet another fine piece of slickrock to practice your Moab skills. Descend off the ridge to the Gashouse Gulch Trail **(15.7)** and turn right on Gashouse. Descend to Miller Gulch Road **(16.3)** and turn right a short distance to the Homestead Trail which can be found on your left. A quick climb puts you at Charlie's Cutoff again. If you want to do Charlie's again, do it, but turn left at the Homestead Trail which will swing you back to the familiar four-way trail intersection. If not doing Charlie's again, drop off the ridge and fly back to the four-way trail intersection **(17.1)**. Continue straight, now on the relocated Strawberry Jack Trail and descend all the way back to Pine Valley after getting some wonderful air on the way back.

TRAIL OPTION: Some riders prefer to do the climbing on the Strawberry Jack Trail as opposed to the Buck Gulch Trail. Give it a whirl.

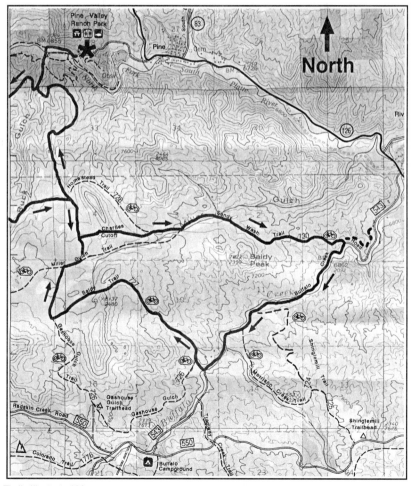

DISTANCE: 7.6 miles

PHYSICAL: ❂❂❨

TECHNICAL: ❂❂❨

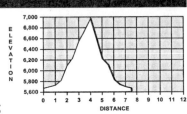

TERRAIN: Pavement; gravel road; scree; loose rocks

GAIN: 1,350 feet

MAPS: Eldorado Canyon State Park

If you are looking for a nice, easy ride, avoid this trail. If you want a long, fast ride, avoid this trail. But, if your desires are for a short steep, technical outing on the all too frequent loose rock, give it a shot. The single track climb out of South Boulder Creek is stiff and intense; 1,000 feet in two miles and at times has the feel that you are riding on marbles. Recent trail maintenance has made the climb somewhat easier than in the past. Have I scared you off? Bring some money since there is a small fee to enter Eldorado State Park.

ACCESS: To get to this southern Boulder ride, take Colorado 93 out of Golden to Eldorado Springs Drive and turn left towards the State Park for just over 1.7 miles. Turn left into the Doudy Draw trailhead parking lot.

DESCRIPTION: Get back on Eldorado Springs Drive, turning left, and head to the State Park entrance **(1.4).** Continue up the gravel road for about 0.6 miles to the Fowler Trailhead **(2.0)** and turn left onto the singletrack. The signed Rattlesnake Gulch Trail splits right from the Fowler Trail just 0.2 miles from the start of the singletrack. This is where the fun begins. Start scrambling up over/around/through the rock water bars and the frequently loose rocks. As the trail finally smooths and the grade flattens, find yourself at the Crags Hotel ruin **(3.3).** Continue towards the Continental Divide Overlook and keep cranking steeply uphill to the south until you reach the high point **(4.1)** which is nearly upon some railroad tracks. The trail turns left and sharply down over very loose rocks and completes the loop **(4.4)** at the Crags Hotel ruin. Turn right, backtracking, and careful fly back down to the start using your best downhill skills.

TRAIL OPTION: Because of it relatively short distance, this ride is best done from Boulder by combining this ride with the Community Ditch and Marshall Mesa trails. The Marshall/Community/Rattlesnake combo will be approximately 16 miles.

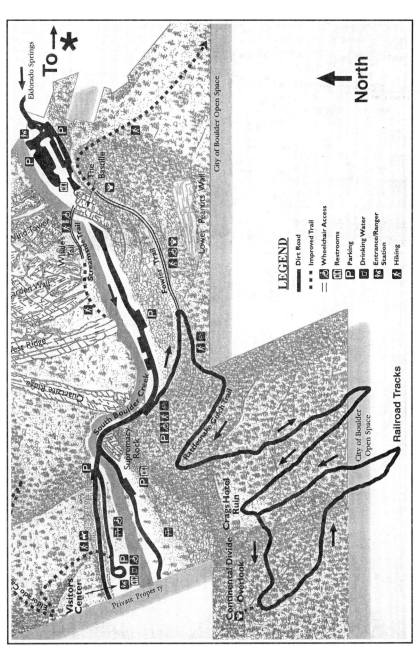

LEGEND

- ▬▬ Dirt Road
- ▪▪▪ Improved Trail
- ═ Wheelchair Access
- 🚻 Restrooms
- 🅿 Parking
- 🚰 Drinking Water
- 🏠 Entrance/Ranger Station
- 🚶 Hiking

To → Eldorado Springs

← North

The Bastille
Lower Peanuts Wall
City of Boulder Open Space
Vird Tower
Whale's Tail
Streamside Trail
Garden Wall
West Ridge
Quartzite Ridge
Fowler Trail
South Boulder Creek
Supremacy Rock
Rattlesnake Gulch Trail
Crags Hotel Ruin
Continental Divide Overlook
City of Boulder Open Space
Railroad Tracks
Visitors Center
Private Property

RIDE 19 RINGTAIL TRAIL

DISTANCE: 15.8 miles

PHYSICAL: ⊙⊙⊙

TECHNICAL: ⊙⊙

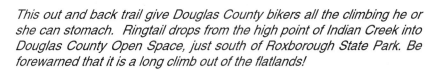

TERRAIN: Solid to loose single track. A few rocks

GAIN: 3,900 feet

MAPS: Trails Illustrated - Deckers/Rampart Range

This out and back trail give Douglas County bikers all the climbing he or she can stomach. Ringtail drops from the high point of Indian Creek into Douglas County Open Space, just south of Roxborough State Park. Be forewarned that it is a long climb out of the flatlands!

ACCESS: Drive South on US 85 (Santa Fe Drive) to Sedalia and turn right on Colorado 67. Follow Colorado 67 for about 10 miles to the Indian Creek Campground, just past Rampart Range Road. Turn right and park near the restroom. There may be a day use fee so bring some dollars.

DESCRIPTION: Spot the single track Indian Creek Trail (Trail #800) and begin climbing north from the parking lot. Pop out on to Forest Road 512 **(1.6)**. Find the start of the Ringtail Trail across the road. Ringtail climbs stiffly, but quickly to the ridge summit **(1.9)**. Roll up and down along the ridge for a while where the trail then begins a more consistent and fairly fast drop. Enter Douglas County Open space and pass an old cabin **(4.3)** on your right. As you enter into scrub oak, the trail turns south a short distance before heading east, then north all the while continuing to lose elevation. Stay on the well used trail as several trail spurs are found. Encounter some switchbacks just before finally arriving at the valley floor. Continue to head north until you encounter Swallowtail Trail **(7.5)**. Keep left now on Swallowtail, passing a second Swallowtail spur before pedaling to a gate within sight of County Road 5. From here back track the way you came enjoying the "fun" grunt back to the top.

TRAIL OPTION: Checkout the short Swallowtail Trail loop that you passed - it is a really sweet trail.

Trails Illustrated Map

DISTANCE: 9.7 miles

PHYSICAL: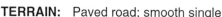

TECHNICAL: ○

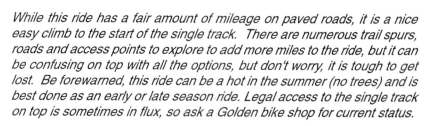

TERRAIN: Paved road; smooth single and two-track; frequent rocky sections

GAIN: 1,060 feet

MAP: USGS - Golden

While this ride has a fair amount of mileage on paved roads, it is a nice easy climb to the start of the single track. There are numerous trail spurs, roads and access points to explore to add more miles to the ride, but it can be confusing on top with all the options, but don't worry, it is tough to get lost. Be forewarned, this ride can be a hot in the summer (no trees) and is best done as an early or late season ride. Legal access to the single track on top is sometimes in flux, so ask a Golden bike shop for current status.

ACCESS: Find your way to downtown Golden and park. The ride begins across the street from the Coors Brewery at Ford and 13th Street.

DESCRIPTION: Head east on 13th Street for one block to East Street, turn right and start your climb. Cross and turn left on to South Golden Rd. **(1.0)**. At the first traffic circle, cross over to West 16th Ave. and continue to climb **(1.5)**. Turn left onto Golden Hills Drive **(1.9)** which will turn right after 1 block and continue climbing on Golden Hills Drive. Just as you descend off the crest of the hill, spy the single track on your left **(2.3)** between several rocks and just before Quaker Street. Climb on this single-track trail to where the trail cross a two-track **(2.8)**. Turn left on the two-track and head west on the sometimes rocky trail. Under the powerline, the trail heads north and continues to climb. As the trail crosses under the powerline **(4.2)** stay right and head for the obvious Castle Rock **(4.5)** which makes for a great lunch stop. Backtrack a short distance from Castle Rock, take the second left trail spur and steeply climb a short distance to where the trail joins yet another spur **(4.7)**. Veer right and go under the powerline which begins the decent portion of the ride. The trail joins a two-track road **(5.3)** and continues east. Near several confusing trial junctions **(5.8)** continue straight on single track and do a fun short loop. After completing the loop, turn right then quickly left and cross back over the two-track road **(6.5)**. The trail now drops towards the south and to the start of the main loop **(6.9)** which should look familiar. Continue descending the way you came where the single track fun ends all too quick back at Golden Hills Drive **(7.4)**. Turn right and head on back to town.

TRAIL OPTION: I purposely left out several trails spurs on the north and south side for you to explore. Enjoy.

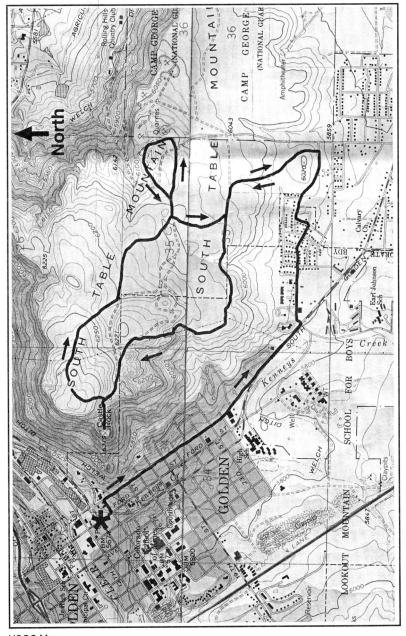

DISTANCE: 6.9 miles

PHYSICAL: ⊙ℂ

TECHNICAL: ⊙ℂ

TERRAIN: Wide to narrow hardpack; some sand and very few rocks

GAIN: 970 feet

MAPS: Jefferson County Open Space - South Valley

Unlike many of the Jeffco Parks, this ride has no extended climbs. Yes, you will get your vertical elevation numbers in as it bobs, rolls and weaves around the spectacular red rock formations and hogback. With the multiple trailheads and access points, this park allows you to get creative and so your ride can be different every time. Combined with road or paved path miles, this can be as long or as short as one desires and is also a good winter ride. There may be seasonal closures on some trails.

ACCESS: From C470, exit at Kipling Street and head south, then quickly west following the signs toward Deer Creek Canyon Park, but not to Deer Creek Canyon Park. Just prior to South Valley Road, spy the parking and trailhead on your right. Another larger trailhead can be found on the north side the park off of South Valley Road.

DESCRIPTION: Begin climbing on the wide Coyote Song Trail. Note where a narrow single-track trail joins **(0.4)** the trail - you will take this trail on the way back. Continue climbing and turn right on Lyons Back Trail **(0.9)**. Quickly "climb" the stairs and find yourself at the ridge summit. Pass two spur trails on your left and right as you descend off the summit now on the Pass Trail. Take the first right in the swale below to the wide, two track road, known as Cathy Johnson Trail **(1.4)**. Turn left and climb on the two-track to the Loop Trail **(2.0)**. Turn left on the Loop Trail and head on back to the ridge summit **(2.6)**. Descent back to Coyote Song Trail, turn left and drop back to the narrow single track trail on your right that you previously passed **(3.1)**. Drop down to the wide Swallow Song Trail **(3.4)**, turn left and follow it all the way down to South Valley Road **(3.7)**. Cross the road and pickup Grazing Elk Trail. Quickly climb up to the mesa to the start of a loop **(4.0)**. I like doing the loop counter clockwise, so turn right and climb for about a mile before starting a fun descent through several ravines and back to the start of the loop **(6.3)**. Turn right and head back to South Valley Road, where you turn right and drop back to the start of the ride **(6.9)**.

TRAIL OPTIONS: A. Join this ride with Deer Creek Canyon Park for a very nice combination of mileage, scenery and different type of trails. There is now a nice connector trail, Rattlesnake Gulch, from the Grazing Elk Trail loop over to the Deer Creek Canyon Park parking lot. **B.** There are a couple of nice unmarked spur trails off the top of Lyons Back Trail. My favorite is the one that races south off the divide down to the Cathy Johnson Trail - watch out for the corners!

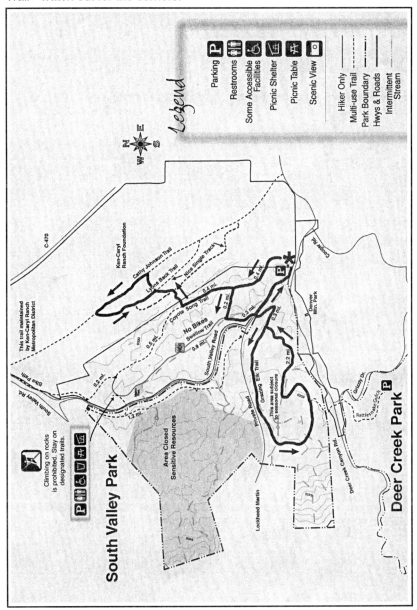

RIDE 22 STEVENS GULCH

DISTANCE: 10.0 miles

PHYSICAL: ⚙⚙⚙

TECHNICAL: ⚙⚙

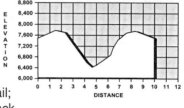

TERRAIN: Forest road; primitive trail; narrow to wide single track

GAIN: 2,000 feet

MAPS: Trails Illustrated - Deckers/Rampart Range

This new loop gives Douglas County residents some fine, yet primitive single track closer to home. Some hiking with your bike should be expected on this primitive and sometimes steep trail. This ride also provides many ride options with the Indian Creek Trail and Roxborough Loop connections close by. This ride and the options are waiting for you and your knobbies.

ACCESS: Drive South on US 85 (Santa Fe Drive) to Sedalia and turn right on Colorado 67. Follow Colorado 67 for about 10 miles to the Indian Creek Campground, just past Rampart Range Road. Turn right and park near the restroom. There may be a day use fee so bring some dollars.

DESCRIPTION: Spot the single track Indian Creek Trail (Trail #800) and begin climbing north from the parking lot. Pop out on to Forest Road 512 **(1.6)** and veer left on this road still on Trail 800. Follow the road to a 4-way intersection **(2.3)** and take the left road split as it sharply drops into aspens. This road eventually becomes two-track and is a fast and fun descent along Stevens Gulch. As you pass an old cabin on your left, the trail joins with another **(4.2)**. Go right and continue a beautiful decent passing more cabins **(4.5)**. Just after you pass these cabins **(4.7)**, a trail takes off on your right. Take this trail and begin a short climb where the trail comes to a 4-way intersection **(5.0)**. Take the trail split that heads south and slightly downhill to a small brook. Cross this brook several times as the trail becomes less pronounced and follows the west side of the brook towards the south, uphill all the way. After crossing a side creek **(6.1)** that may be dry, look right and spot the optional trail to the top as it climbs steeply on the nose of a ridge where walking is likely. Most riders should continue on the main trail to a small meadow under the powerline. After a tough switchback the trail becomes a road and then quickly joins another road. Turn left a short distance, still climbing, where you quickly climb to a T intersection **(7.6)**. Go right at this intersection and climb back to the 4-way **(8.3)** completing the loop. From here back track the way you came, enjoying the fun singletrack drop to the parking area.

TRAIL OPTIONS: A. This ride can be done in the opposite direction which will make for easy climbing out of Stevens Gulch and a more difficult downhill ride. **B.** Both the Indian Creek Trail and Roxborough Loop can easily be accessed. Highly consider taking Indian Creek back to the start.

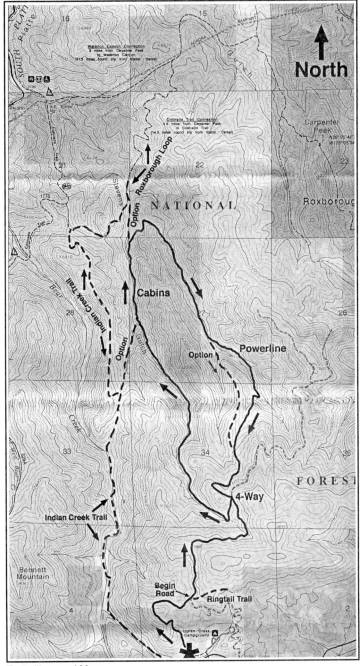

TRAIL NOTES AND CHANGES

Several trails have purposely been omitted from this guide book. A brief reason for omitting the trails follows.

1. Roxborough State Park. Mountain biking is not permitted on trails within the park, with the exception of the "Power Line" Trail on the westside of the park. This trail (#800) is now part of the Indian Creek Loop that can be accessed from either Waterton Canyon or from the Indian Creek Campground.

2. Long Scraggy Ride. This ride was in previous editions of this guide, but unfortunately this ride was a casualty of the 1996 Buffalo Creek Fire/Flood with Trail 695 now permanently closed. However, an easy forest road ride along Dell Gulch still exists. See ride number 4 in this book for directions.

3. O'Fallon Park. The City of Denver closed all the trails to mountain bikers in 2002 except the Bear Creek corridor trail. This small park had some stellar, rarely used trails that the Kittredge locals are gonna miss.

4. Reynolds Park. Jeffco Open Space has closed this park to mountain bikers due to lack of use. While not the most popular ride in the Front Range, it had some a nice fun trails that will be missed.

5. Cherry Creek State Park. While there is still some nice single track left on the south side of the park, much of the original single track through the wetlands is off-limits.

6. Chatfield State Park. Too many goatheads and not enough singletrack.

7. Bear Creek Lake Park. Some informal short trails along with goatheads.

8. Mud Lake. This new Boulder County Open Space just north of Nederland along Hwy 72 has some nice short loops to explore.

If anyone has trail suggestions for future updates to this guide, please contact me with your thoughts and comments. Write or email me at:

Tom "Barn" Barnhart
Fat Tire Press
P.O. Box 620283,
Littleton, CO 80162

barno@excite.com

MOUNTAIN BIKING CLUBS

Colorado Mountainbike Association and Boulder Mountainbike Alliance are great clubs that helps to maintain existing trails and develops new ones. This is a great way to meet new riders and a way to give something back to the sport of mountain biking. Please consider joining COMBA or BMA.

**For more information
visit our web site at:
www.boa-mtb.org/**

**The Boulder Off-Road Alliance
exists to serve as a positive
voice for mountain biking in
the Boulder County region.**

For more information visit COMBA's web site at:
www.comba.org

If you want the best, custom mountain bike available on the planet checkout the maker of my bike.

www.sevencycles.com

Not Front Range, but part of Colorado

Bobcat on the prowl